CW00590454

THE
CHAMBER
OF CELEBRITY PA SECRETS

VIP

Donna Coulling

THE
CHAMBER
OF CELEBRITY PA SECRETS

ENDORSEMENTS

DONNA COULLING HAS BEEN MY personal assistant for thirteen years and secretly I wish that she'll stay forever because I'm not sure I could function without her. Everyone should have a Donna in their lives. She is my fairy godmother: every wish gets granted. From filing, correspondence, bills, and dealing with the monotonous and never-ending maintenance of house and household, from fixing everything that breaks down -making up for all my incompetence

(Particularly in the breaking down department) Ocado, pet sitting, there is little that Donna cannot do. Superdon is her nickname. She is supersonically efficient, - I've never had to ask her to do anything twice, in fact I barely have to ask once before its done, she has thoughtful initiative, is consistently cheery, has a lovely manner with people, utterly professional in a job where lines could get blurred, fun, discreet, and basically perfect. I would trust her with my life. In fact I do.

Helena Bonham Carter

DONNA IS A TROUBLE-SHOOTER. She thinks of everything that could possibly go wrong BEFORE it goes wrong, and that's what makes her great. She is always full of good cheer and pep, and organises everything with charm and ease and total professionalism. She keeps many balls in the air at the same time, and makes it look effortless (which of course it isn't). She is a total joy to work with and I count myself very lucky to have her in my life.

Rachel Weisz

The Chamber
of Celebrity PA Secrets

VIP

Donna Coulling

The Chamber of Celebrity PA Secrets
©2014 Donna Coulling

eISBN: 978-1-62020-327-9

Cover Design by Joshua Frederick, Ambassador
International Digital
Book Design by Anna Riebe, Ambassador
International Digital

AMBASSADOR INTERNATIONAL
427 Wade Hampton Blvd
Greenville, SC 29609, USA
800-209-8570
www.ambassador-international.com

TABLE OF CONTENTS

DEDICATION

For my Minx, my light, my soul, my inspiration.

Ladyboss - love and laughter.

WITH THANKS

To those clients I have had the opportunity to work with and learn from. To the PA's I have met along the way who have been so generous with their experiences and knowledge - You're all awesome, believe in yourselves and let's continue to support each other and take over the world!

PART
ONE

ANYONE CAN BE A CELEBRITY

PERSONAL ASSISTANT, RIGHT?

I BECAME A CELEBRITY ASSISTANT because of my background as an actor. I worked as an actor, and then I didn't work much as an actor . . . So, I started working for actors!

I don't work for actors because I want to be their best friend and seen in magazines with them. I don't work for actors because I want to be tripping down a red carpet every other week, falling out of nightclubs, or whatever else you imagine they do from the information you're fed from the newspapers.

I work for them because I feel I know the industry. Much like a legal secretary trains to work in a law firm and a medical secretary studies to work in a doctor's surgery or hospital: we all learn the foundations of the industry we work within. That's exactly what I did.

When I started, I had no idea this job existed—no clue at all. I trained at the Italia Conti Academy in London and assumed I'd have a heady career in theatre, television, and film. Why else not . . . That's why you go to drama school after all, isn't it?

I loved everything: straight acting, improvisation, and musical theatre. Basically, anything that meant I was at the front of the stage. Prior to going to Conti's, whilst still at school, I worked at the local theatre in Maidstone, Kent where I was an assistant stage manager (ASM) on Dick Whittington, the pantomime that year. Eighty performances and a lot of laughter later, and it was back to class for me.

I also worked at the local television studios—TVS at that time—which meant sitting in on local news shows and watching a lot from behind the camera. After leaving school, I went to work at a holiday camp in Weston Super Mare, which involved everything and anything: calling bingo; ballroom dancing with guests; running the questionable Thursday night competition 'Hunk of the Week'; working backstage on the sound and lights for visiting cabarets, plus introducing cabaret acts; as well as being a dancer in the Bluecoat shows twice a week. I loved performing. When I left, I went straight to Italia Conti to start its Performing Arts course.

Three years later, I was trawling the West End and regional theatres for work, auditioning for anything that had a female of around twenty years old in it. Mostly, I didn't get cast because:

A.   There were a lot of other female twenty-something actors I was up against, and

B.   I was probably a bit rubbish.

I had a day job working on the promotions team for Estee Lauder in department stores in the West End. Most of us who worked there were actors and would skip off if we had an audition in the hope we could get a reprieve from spraying perfume on people for at least a couple of days.

I did some touring theatre out of town—Edinburgh Festival a few times, some fringe shows in London, but nothing of much note. I'd started working at the Actors Centre in Covent Garden, which runs amazing classes and has a fantastic social scene, which I quickly became part of. However, a lot of the actors, who came to take classes or hang out in the café/bar, felt so different to me.

They brimmed, literally over-flowed with confidence. They knew how to work a room, make sure they were seen by the right people, and could talk the talk; loudly, most of the time! I was no good at that. I didn't have much self-confidence and really didn't feel I could contribute, as I hadn't worked enough to feel worthy to be part of this group or their conversations. In essence, networking scared the living daylights out of me.

Although, working there taught me how to use the computer—albeit the basics—prior to that, I'd taken a book out of the library to teach myself how to type. I was far too grand to do anything secretarial at school, of course. So, when a job came up in a talent agency I thought: *what have I got to lose?* I went for it.

I had the actor mentality of "I can do anything." So long as I get the job, I'll learn.

Scuba dive? . . . Of course! Fire-eating? . . . No problem!

When Barry of the Barry Burnet Organisation (now Burnett Crowther Ltd.) asked if I had information technology (IT) skills, I said as I laughed confidently, "Of course!"

"When can you start . . . Tomorrow?" he asked. "Okay, you've got the job."

What!

So I had to quickly organise and started the next day at the agency based at the Prince of Wales Theatre. I really threw myself into the job. I learnt more computer skills, developed a rapport with the actors we looked after, and grew more confident in suggesting them for roles. I went to television recordings and the theatre with casting directors, and built relationships with them.

I was on the telephone constantly learning about what the actors needed when they'd get a role on something—what was required: contracts, riders, per diems, etc. I absorbed everything like a sponge and pretty much forgot all about my performing career as I was enjoying learning about this side of the business and being challenged everyday by what was thrown at me.

I was also networking without trying very hard—on the telephone and by going to the theatre. I grew in confidence, and possibly maturity, and didn't feel so unsure of myself anymore.

After three and a half years, I'd reached the ceiling of the role I had within the company. I could either decide to stay there and do what I was doing for the rest of my days or find something that would challenge me again. I've always loved movies and desperately wanted to work in the movie business. So, I started putting out my feelers.

I found something that sounded interesting and left Barry for a company based in Victoria called IAC Holdings—executive producers of films including: *Nora*, *Shiner*, and the television series *Highlander*. This role was personal assistant (PA) to three producers, who needed someone to do lots of fast typing, and take dictation and shorthand really quickly. I'd never done either, so I made up my own shorthand and dictation.

However, I made no set visits or met anyone remotely movie star related. I realised rapidly it was not the job for me. Thirteen weeks later, more leaving drinks were organised.

Then, I went for a job back in the West End as production secretary on *The Graduate*—a big hit at that time. I'd missed Kathleen Turner as the first Mrs. Robinson and started just after Jerry Hall went in as the second Mrs. Robinson. It was a great show with a lot of brilliant reviews and advance bookings. I was working in the production office on Greek Street, in the heart of Soho.

When I started, I didn't have a computer, so I shared. I had a lot of filing to do and a lot of shopping for the office. I also made coffee, which I don't mind. Everyone has to start somewhere. Yet, after a few months and not seeing much change, I wasn't feeling at all challenged, but I didn't really know where to go next. I'd been in an agency, a film company, and a theatre production company. Yet, I wasn't anywhere near satisfied. I didn't have any specific qualifications apart from a performing arts diploma from Italia Conti and a bit of experience.

I thought about what skills I'd gleaned over the years. I knew I was organised—I practically did that in my sleep. I knew I liked being around actors and I had a good knowledge of theatre and film. I didn't want to work in an office from 9:00–6:00, tied to a desk, waiting for the telephone to ring and looking for things to do. I like to be mentally tested, and I thrive on being busy. So, I know, I'll make up a job!

I put together a curriculum vitae (CV) and cover letter to offer my services as a freelance PA for actors living in the United Kingdom (UK) or travelling in from overseas to shoot here for a few months. I could set them up with a home, driver, nutritionist, yoga teacher, or nanny—anything. In reality, I had no clue, but thought I'd put it out there what I imagined they'd need. I sent my details to twelve talent agents in London.

Unfortunately, one of the responses went to my boss in *The Graduate* office as my name had been typed incorrectly in the email, so he found out I was looking to leave. *Oops!* I needed to make this work.

Top tip: when looking for a new job, use your personal email.

Fortunately, for the first time in my life, timing was on my side. Helena Bonham Carter's current assistant was looking to go travelling; her agent passed my letter on. I met the assistant for wine, and then met Helena for tea. She asked me what I could do. "Anything and everything!" "Okay, deal! Let's start

next week and see how it goes." "Eek!" I'd only gone
and   got   the   job!

EXERCISE:

I believe we all do something for a reason, even those weird and wonderful jobs you may have done as a student for cash will stand you in good stead today. Be it the contacts you made, the things you learned, or just to know you never want to make another donut in your life. Yep, that was one of my jobs!

Think of a list of jobs you've had and write the positives you gained from each of them (however small they may seem).

EXERCISE:

The reason I work for actors and celebrities is because, as I said earlier, I was once an actor. I trained and worked as an actor, and then at a talent agency and for production companies. It's the business I know. When I was at drama school, a singing teacher used to say, "It's your business to know your business." We would all roll our eyes.

I know now what this means and use it repeatedly as a mantra in my training sessions. It's what makes us useful and worth our weight in gold to the people for whom we work. Be it your interest and knowledge in your industry, the passion you have for everything involved with it. Is it sport? Is it law . . . Medicine . . . Finance? Or are you similar to me and it *is* the business of show?

It's your business to know your business. What business do you know?

PART
TWO

WHERE TO FIND WORK WITHOUT

LOOKING LIKE A STALKER.

You have to remember the job of being a celebrity PA is not your everyday job advertised in the media section of *The Guardian* or something a recruitment agency may post on one of its job boards. After meeting with several recruitment agencies over the years, I've learnt if the job for someone high profile comes to them, it's usually because it's done the rounds and nobody can place anybody in it. Reading between the lines: "It's a difficult post to fill" if you know what I mean.

I'm a bit of a jump in feet first type of gal. Due to my previous career, I have a lot of waitressing skills. So, I figure I'll always work if something doesn't quite go to plan. I'm also a believer in if you don't try, you'll never know. So, if you want to take a chance at this job, you can't put up too many boundaries and stipulations. You have to ultimately go for it.

HOW DO YOU CONTACT ACTORS?

Write to them at their homes? Big, fat no. You'll appear to be a stalker. Besides, who do you think opens their mail? That's right, their current assistant.

Unless that assistant is looking to move on, your letter is going to go straight into the shredder.

A lot of actors, as well as everyday people like you and me, are wary of whom to trust—to come into and work inside their homes, to know everything about their private lives and all the dealings that come with that. So, many choose to employ a member of their family. Maybe a sister, cousin, aunt, or an old school friend—someone they know and feel comfortable with. Failing that—or when that person moves on due to relocation, starting a family, or a career change— they may turn to their agent or manager.

The relationship between an actor and his or her agent/manager is a very close one. It is usually a long-standing friendship/relationship. The person is someone the actor trusts implicitly with his or her work and financial dealings. This person usually gets them the best deal, after all. So, they can also be the person they'd ask if they were looking to take on an assistant.

I know a lot of assistants who come from a talent agency background. It's almost like doing a foundation course in being a PA to an actor; you learn everything about them and what comes with the job without the actual hands-on part.

I wrote to talent agencies regularly at the start, as I've always had clients who would have only needed me part-time. Then, when I got my first job, I still needed to fill my week with others. I would write every six weeks, telling them who I was currently working for and that I still had time in my week if they had clients who needed help.

Perseverance – Keep on going, which I know is especially tough when you get nothing back. Yet, keep thinking of your end goal.

Timing – If you don't keep trying, then the one time your email could land in their inbox at that opportune moment may be lost.

Again, be prepared to find another part-time role until you get the ultimate job for which you're looking for.

RESEARCH, RESEARCH, AND MORE RESEARCH.

What you need to think about for that first job.

Yes, I'm a fan of jumping in feet first, but you also have to be practical. I live in the middle of London, so it made sense for me to look for clients here. You have to think seriously what your boundaries are and how you can make yourself as efficient as you can be in your working day.

Location: where do you live?

If you live in a tiny village, there is no point looking to work in the city if you don't want to travel every day. Keep it local and find out who lives near to you—if you are happy to travel, then great. However, also factor in your travel expenses and how you can utilise your time whilst travelling in and out (i.e., calls in the car, emails on the train) or whether you only want to work two or three days a week in the city and stay with a friend to save on expensive travel costs.

There is a lot of work that can be done virtually, which is not necessarily in a physical office location. Work you can take home with you—as long as you have access to your telephone and email—can be completed from anywhere.

Fact – Not all actors and celebrities live in a city. So, don't narrow it down to thinking you have to live in a major city.

If you do live out of town, then, perhaps, there are actors who have a country home near you if not a permanent home from where they may like someone to work. By the power of the local telegraph, and everyone knowing each others business, it's not hard to find out if someone high profile is living nearby.

Don't write to them at home – Instead, look up their agent via a professional service such as—if you're in the UK—www.spotlight.com and drop them an email with your details, making a point of telling them you're local. This is your unique selling point (USP) above other people who may be writing in also.

If you're unsure of who your local people of interest are who you might want to work for, how about looking at nearby bookshops and libraries for anyone giving talks or book readings. Don't limit yourself to just actors. Also think of all the poets, authors, playwrights, entrepreneurs, etc. who work from home and need PA help, too.

The list is plentiful. You can meet some truly fabulously interesting people out there.

Is there a theatre near you? Could there be any work there to enable you to meet people or, at least, be in the right environment to hear of work? Maybe box office, administrative staff, front of house, etc.? Maybe there are touring productions where an actor may be appearing for a couple of months, particularly around Christmas when it's pantomime time. The bigger regional theatres usually get a star performer for their productions, who will be based locally for a time and may need some assistance.

Are there any local production companies you can try to meet with and talk to? Perhaps, they're filming something nearby and need a runner or a PA to help out. It's all experience, which enables you to meet other like-minded people in the industry.

Also, at a local radio station it does tend to be a case of who you know. If you don't get yourself out there to meet people, then no one will ever know you're there.

Motivation – If you really want to get your dream job, you have to keep going. Don't leave any stone unturned.

CARPE DIEM – SEIZE THE DAY!

What to put in that first email and on your CV.

Your agent email needs to be short and to the point. They receive a gazillion emails a day and won't have time to read your life story or funny witticisms you might think will make you stand out from the rest. State clearly what you're offering, your location, and availability.

Of course, be polite. Manners go a long way and these people really don't owe you a favour nor have they been waiting their whole lives to read your email. However, it may just land at that opportune moment as they've put the telephone down to a client who has asked, "Do you know someone who could PA for me?"

Is your CV relevant for the roles you want?

Yes, I'm certain you have software skills, leadership experience, and planned corporate events until you're blue in the face. Yet, if you're looking to land a private/celebrity PA role, these aren't the skills for which your prospective boss will be ultimately looking.

Event planning is great, as there may be family, private, and pre- and after-parties; book readings/signings, etc., depending on the role. So, word your event planning in a way your potential client might think about how they can use your experience.

What personal tasks have you incorporated into your current role that can transfer into a private role? Remember, the majority of assistants will work from their boss' homes, so it's imperative to word your skills in a way that adapts to an office, or kitchen table in a home, rather than in a global organisation.

IT and software skills are essential, as a lot of the time you'll be the IT department when things go wrong.

Leading a team can be useful also, but more so working as part of a team. You may be a great team leader, but a great team member is much more employable.

Think of the differences between a private and corporate PA when writing up your CV. Imagine you're the client: which skills will you look for in a PA?

EVERY DAY IS DIFFERENT.

I love that they are. I love not knowing what I'm walking into and the challenges I can be thrown. One day I can be a personal shopper; the next day, project manager; the next day, event planner; the next day, gofer; and so the list goes on.

When I came to the job and I knew no one and nothing, I thought I had absolutely no skills whatsoever. However, then I thought about the skills I have that I use at home and in everyday life: insurance claims, changing a fuse, administrative tasks, banking, researching repair companies, taking the car to the garage, rebooting the WiFi, online shopping, and many more.

These are skills we forget we have. Yet, when you're looking to work within a private home and closely with an individual, these are skills you will be using every single day.

The three great essentials to achieve anything

worthwhile are, first, hard work;

second, stick-to-itiveness; third, common sense.

—Thomas A. Edison

I HAD MY FIRST GIG, NOW I NEEDED

TO GET MY SECOND, BUT HOW?

So, I had my first client, but she only needed me two days a week. This can be common in the UK for actors, unless they have a production company, write or direct, or head a charity, etc. I'd just resigned from a full-time position and I needed to fill the rest of my week and quickly.

I was now able to re-write my CV and incorporate what I was doing in my new job—I was, after all, officially a celebrity PA. Then, I did the same as I've just recommended you do to get your first job. I emailed all those agents and production companies every six weeks, telling them of the one client I had and that I had time to work for some more.

I also took on a part-time office job to supplement my income until I managed to build up my client base. It was about perseverance, patience, and not pushing my luck (i.e. annoying agents by contacting them too often).

Some clients you may work for might only need you for a few months while they're working on a film or a specific project. However, even if it's not full-time or a permanent role, it's all great experience and you're building on who you know, which may lead to another job.

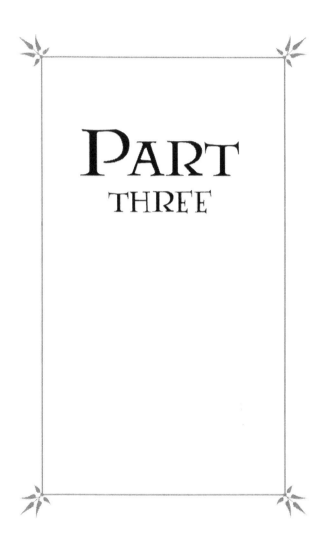

PART
THREE

I GOT THE JOB. . . NOW, WHAT DO I DO?

Congratulations, you got the job!

Now, you'll find there are a ton of other people out there who want your job, too, so it's down to you to be the best at what you do.

I believe people evolve every day, and this job is ideal for that. Every day is completely different; you'll be thrown numerous curveballs and wake in the night sweating, thinking: *did I reserve/cancel that booking for tomorrow morning?* Of course, you won't do that often as you'll be fabulous in your new job, but we're only human after all.

This is a job without a regular job description. You may have interviewed for your position via an agency or referral and seen a basic job spec. You and I both know this is a very *basic* job description. If you were given the *real* job description it would be something completely different.

Think back to your last role, if you haven't been in this one very long, and imagine you're taking a sabbatical for a year. You need to find someone to fill your shoes for that time. From what you've learnt from doing this job for a time, for the VIP, CEO, or whoever what would that difference in job description be?

Now you can see the 'real' job description—the nitty-gritty, everyday "predict the future" role you manage to keep on top of every day:

You can see from how much more you do than was originally asked of you: working for more than one person, longer hours, knowing your boss' preferences, knowing him or her inside and out. Being a crystal ball reader, making a sow's ear into a silk purse, juggling several balls at once and the list goes on.

KEEPING THREE STEPS AHEAD

To me, one or two steps mostly aren't enough; you have to keep three steps ahead at all times. Being able to predict what your client might need and what could possibly go wrong before he or she knows what he or she wants, but will want you to suggest options before he or she even knew what he or she needs, and then changing his or her mind once you've put everything in place!

So long as you always think of the worse-case scenario—what could possibly go wrong—and then work back from there and have a back-up plan in place, everything should go swimmingly. Other than that, we are human and they are human, too. We all make mistakes: take responsibility for your mistakes and learn from them.

Putting personal systems in place does no harm at all. Whether it's only checking emails at certain times during the day, writing a list the night before for the next day, or first thing in the morning so you have your to-do tasks to concentrate on straight away. Use whatever systems you find to remain on top and three steps ahead.

I like to respond to emails in the evenings while I'm watching television. If they require simple yes, no, or I'll check tomorrow responses, I'm happy to clear those from inbox rather than wake up to a lot of questions the next morning.

We all work in different ways and have tried and tested methods for doing things. Don't be afraid to incorporate ways you've used in the past in your new role if you know it will make you more efficient. They'll thank you later.

WHERE AND WHAT ARE THE

BOUNDARIES, AND HOW DO I

ADHERE TO THEM?

By having no job description, plus working from someone's private home, there can be a lot of grey areas.

For me, it's easy I remember he or she is the employer and I'm the employee. Yes, I know a lot about the employer and vice versa, but I always respect—at the end of the day—he or she is my boss and the one paying my wages.

It's a very close personal relationship being someone's PA. I do joke that we've done births, deaths, and marriages between us; yet, it's true. However, that doesn't mean I can push the boundaries. There is a lot of responsibility with the role and a lot will be expected of you. You have to ask questions to be able to do your job the best you can, but not too many questions to become irritating and make the client think: I *may as well do it myself.*

Personality is everything when you're working so closely with someone and knowing when to be quiet. I go into someone's home stealth, as I don't know what I'm walking into. He or she really doesn't need someone charging in with a trumpet fanfare—you need to be able to work together. In the same way, you can't bring your *baggage* to work with you either. Of course, there are times when you may be feeling a bit low or fragile, the same way your boss may be, too. So, be respectful of the quieter times.

We all have up, down, busy, and distracted days and so on. This you have to respect when working in a private home, as this is that person's home: their sanctuary, their safe place where they can be themselves and not have to put on an act for others. Remember that and don't take everything personally.

MAINTAINING A GOOD WORKING

RELATIONSHIP

To maintain a good working relationship, I see it the same as maintaining any other friendship/relationship we have in our lives. The way we treat our peers and friends with respect, thought, and communication is the same way we should treat our working relationships. It has to be two-way or it won't work.

In this same way, if your personalities don't gel, then you can't force it. The same in that you can't force a friendship, you can't force a working relationship. If you clash or don't work in a similar way, then it just may not work out. Try not to take it personally and just put it down to experience.

BE THE "YES AND. . ." PERSON, NOT THE "YES, BUT. . ." PERSON.

None of us wants to work twenty-four hours a day, which I know is hard when we are attached to our Smartphones that scream email and text messages to us every moment. Our lives are fast and furious, and it does feel as though we're on a hamster wheel the majority of the time. This means we need to work out strategies that keep us ahead and are time-saving, too.

Out of all of those tasks/challenges we're thrown on a daily basis, are there some that can be combined? If you're travelling across town to pick things up for a client, can you think ahead and plan to pick up several things on the same trip?

"Yes and . . . What else can I pick up/do you need?"

Rather than:

"Yes, but . . . The traffic will be terrible and it'll take forever, so I won't be able to get that other thing finished, etc."

Part of our job role is being able to manage our time efficiently. If you're like me, I don't always see the people for who I work for a huge length of time, so I have to quickly evaluate what's priority and how I can be more productive in the time I'm physically with them. I have to constantly think ahead all of the time in order to manage that time more effectively.

LITTLE BLACK BOOK OF CONTACTS.

When I came into this job, I really didn't know anything apart from my life and office skills, or anyone. I realised very quickly I needed to build a support network around me. I needed certain numbers on speed dial of people and companies to help me, and fast, when I needed them.

I love a project and I enjoy researching new things. Because of the type of people I worked for from the beginning, I knew I would need help with fashion, beauty, hair, hotels, travel, and restaurants—actually everything! I've lived in London a long time and do enjoy travel, theatre, film, and eating out. So, I had a small knowledge of some of the places my clients may enjoy, but it was very minimal.

This needed work and I had to put together my little black book of contacts. I googled public relations (PR) companies, hotels, restaurants, fashion brands, beauty brands—you name it, I faxed it (hey, it was twelve years ago!). I also asked to be put on their mailing lists for new products, accommodations, and press days. Some did and some didn't.

It was great to be able to reach out to all of these people around me, who were working in luxury brands and starting to build my small network. I would meet people for coffee, lunch, or drinks; some of them are now great friends who I know I can rely on in a moment of crisis. Still, that network continues to grow all the time and I say it again and again: I'm nothing without my little black book of contacts.

This is partly why I started my website: www.donnacoulling.com to recommend and share companies, products, and services I have used for years, just discovered, or have re-discovered—to encourage you to build and share your own black books, too.

A GIFT-WRAPPED SWAN AT

MIDNIGHT...?

People say being a PA must be a lonely job, as you mostly work alone. You're left to your own devices, possibly imagining you can go days without even speaking to someone. What! How could that really happen?

Even before I knew there were other freelance celebrity PA types out there, I have never gone a day without communicating with someone. Some may even say talking to oneself doesn't count. Rubbish! I've had some of my best conversations with myself!

From the start, however, I really wanted to meet other assistants who could share their experiences and contacts with me. I wanted to join associations and organisations, but who and where are they? Well, Google is a great place to start of course.

I found www.nycelebrityassistants.com and www.acpa-la.com, but I don't live in the United States and I wanted to find somewhere closer to home. There wasn't really anything back then, but now there is www.aca-uk.com. As you are now employed as a celebrity PA, you can apply for membership, too.

However, if you're not yet working in your dream role, but are working as a PA, there are many organisations you can still join. Google them and you'll find there are a lot of which you don't even have to pay a membership fee. They run a lot of events, some run online forums if you have questions and need help sourcing a venue, a gift-wrapped swan at midnight, or a private jet.

PAs, in general, are a supportive bunch and we really do want to try to help each other out as much as we can. We're very willing to share resources. Especially, if you find a company or service that has helped you out of a really sticky situation, usually last minute! You'll want to shout its name from the rooftops for everyone else to use.

Join these PA associations, even if you live out of town and can't get to events, you can still share and glean information from their forums, newsletters, and email contact lists to build up your network. And if you can get to an event, even better!

Again, I've met some friends for life through some of these. Yes, some events look painful; I won't lie, but some of the ones you may be dreading turn out to be the really fun nights. As a PA in a major city, you can pretty much be out every weekday evening, if you wanted to be, attending some event or another!

MY NETWORKING TIPS.

Don't get drunk; everyone there is a PA, too. We all represent the person we work for at the end of the day. No one wants to be remembered as "blah blah's assistant is well up for it—they were all over the place at that club opening." Plus, you've usually got to work the next day and you know the day you don't feel great will be one of your most challenging, yet. . .

Think about what you're wearing; we don't want to, but we all judge a book by its cover. I have been to events where people turn up looking as though they've been tending to their gardens all day, which is frightening when you know they've actually been to work like that, too. Even a Friday lunchtime event where it's dress down Friday in the office, doesn't mean dress down at the lunchtime networking event at a major hotel.

Don't worry, not everyone there will know someone either. Think about Anna Wintour, the *Vogue* editor who allegedly goes to some events for ten minutes. Yes, just ten minutes, but the point is she was there. Turn up, greet the host, have a drink of something, look around the room, smile, maybe approach someone who also looks as though they're there alone.

I like to use compliments: "Great bag!" "Great shoes!" or "Do you know this venue/association?" I'll either be snubbed—hopefully not, but it has happened and, frankly, if that's the case they're not worth your time—or thanked for the compliment, which, in turn, starts a conversation. Look, you're building your network!

If you only plan on doing an Anna—just ten minutes—then you're pretty much done at this point. Thank the host and be on your way. Oh, and if you're lucky, there might even be a goody bag!

Follow up; send an email the next day, thanking the host for the evening. Again, another contact in your book—also the venue if you were given those details, too. Another contact, do you see how easy this is? Maybe even the person who had the great shoes! It may not have been the best night out ever, but you might have found an ally for the next time.

WHY BOTHER NETWORKING?

You're building your little black book every time you network. It's another name, company, or service and you never know when the time will come up when you'll fret, "Who was that person who worked for thingy? They'll be able to help me with [insert impossible celebrity PA request].

There may be a time when you're looking to move on from your current role. To either replace *you* or find another job. As I mentioned earlier, these jobs aren't the type you find on a regular job board. They are more word of mouth. If you haven't met anybody, how will you be able to hear of anything that's word of mouth?

Because it's fun and great to meet new people who share a similar interest (i.e., work). There isn't everyone in your life who will understand the trials and tribulations of your everyday job. There are some days when everything doesn't quite go to plan and you really want to vent to someone who will understand. Trust me, you'll meet people when you're networking who will understand those daily challenges we face.

OPPORTUNITIES LAUNCHED BY

YOUR DREAM JOB.

I believe opportunities are given to us in abundance, but it's up to us to acknowledge them and, perhaps, be brave enough to seize them.

I love my job. I'm passionate about my job. I do want to do a Julie Andrews in *The Sound of Music* and sing "The hills are alive . . ." some days because once you find that job:

Choose a job you love, and you will never have to work a day in your life.

Confuciu

s

44

I mentioned I was an actor and was used to working for six weeks at a time if I was lucky. Mostly, I was temping and even though I had a sense of humour about it all, none it was fulfilling or satisfying. I thought I'd made up this job and I'm really glad I did. As over thirteen years later, I'm the happiest I've been and at the end of each day I have an incredible feeling of achievement and job satisfaction.

Strangely, eight years in, I responded to a request from a production company looking for a PA who worked in music. I didn't, but I worked for an ex-music manager, so I emailed and offered to come for a chat if it was helpful. That led to me playing me—'Donna Coulling, celebrity PA'—on a television pilot for Channel 4, then to a 10-part series for Living TV. And as a presenter in my own right I'm regularly seen on QVC UK, infomercials and commercials.

Along with running day courses on being a PA, individual coaching, speaking at PA conferences internationally, running a website and weekly newsletter, and writing this book, I still have my day job. I wouldn't be without it. It's what feeds my curiosity, my soul, it fulfills me, and at the end of the day it feeds me!

Never say never.

DONNA COULLING HAS BEEN PA to Helena Bonham Carter, Rachel Weisz, Sir Derek Jacobi and many other celebrities over the past decade.

She is known as an expert in her field and has made countless television appearances as a celebrity PA and is regularly seen as a guest presenter on the shopping Channel QVC in the UK. She has been featured in many publications and is a popular international public speaker.

www.donnacoulling.com

donna@donnacoulling.com

Twitter: @DCPAGirl

www.facebook.com/donnacoulling

Printed in Great Britain
by Amazon